I0816946

TUNNELS AND PASSAGES

An imprint of Abdo Publishing
abdobooks.com

ANNA ANDERHAGEN

TAKE IT TO THE XTREME!

GET READY FOR AN EXTREME ADVENTURE! THE PAGES OF THIS BOOK WILL TAKE YOU INTO THE WONDROUS WORLD BENEATH YOUR FEET. WHEN YOU HAVE FINISHED READING THIS BOOK, TAKE THE XTREME CHALLENGE ON PAGE 45 ABOUT WHAT YOU'VE LEARNED!

ABDOBOOKS.COM
Published by Abdo Publishing, a division of ABDO, PO Box 398166, Minneapolis, Minnesota 55439.

Printed in the United States of America, North Mankato, MN.
102025
012026

Design: Kelly Doudna, Mighty Media, Inc.
Production: Mighty Media, Inc.
Editor: Katherine Chu

Cover Photograph: Khalil Rabees/Shutterstock
Interior Photographs: ALBINMARCINIAK/Adobe Stock, pp. 30–31; Alina Filatova/Shutterstock, pp. 26–27; Andrea Izzotti/Adobe Stock, pp. 14–15; Anna.Suslina/Adobe Stock, pp. 28–29; Armando Mancini/Wikimedia Commons, p. 44; Cristian Puscasu/Shutterstock, pp. 36–37; Danny Ye/Shutterstock, pp. 20–21; Dirk Wenzel/Adobe Stock, pp. 4–5; dronepicr/Wikimedia Commons, pp. 22–23; Haweb/Wikimedia Commons, pp. 6–7; John M. Wing/Wikimedia Commons, p. 39; Khalil Rabees/Shutterstock, p. 1; Lucille Cottin/Adobe Stock, pp. 12–13; Massimo Santi/Adobe Stock, pp. 32–33; Mikhail Gnatkovskiy/Shutterstock, pp. 10–11; oleg_doroshenko/Adobe Stock, pp. 18–19; onyx/Adobe Stock, pp. 24–25; rabbit75_fot/Adobe Stock, pp. 38–39; Rémi Villalongue/Wikimedia Commons, p. 5; RG72/Wikimedia Commons, p. 19; Salvatore Leanza/Adobe Stock, pp. 34–35; ullstein bild Dtl./Getty Images, pp. 40–41; UrbanImages/Alamy Photo, pp. 42–43; Wikimedia Commons, p. 41; Wyatt Rivard/Shutterstock, pp. 8–9; xuanhuongho/Shutterstock, pp. 16–17
Design Elements: tsayuet/Adobe Stock (rocky texture); Tunatura/Adobe Stock (tunnel texture)

LIBRARY OF CONGRESS CONTROL NUMBER: 2025939068
PUBLISHER'S CATALOGING-IN-PUBLICATION DATA
Names: Anderhagen, Anna, author.
Title: Tunnels and passages / by Anna Anderhagen
Description: Minneapolis, Minnesota : Abdo Publishing, 2026 | Series: Xtreme underground mysteries | Includes online resources and index.
Identifiers: ISBN 9781098297824 (lib. bdg.) | ISBN 9798384930631 (ebook)
Subjects: LCSH: Passages (Corridors)--Juvenile literature. | Archaeology--Juvenile literature. | Geosciences--Juvenile literature. | Earth sciences--Juvenile literature.
Classification: DDC 624.1--dc23

CONTENTS

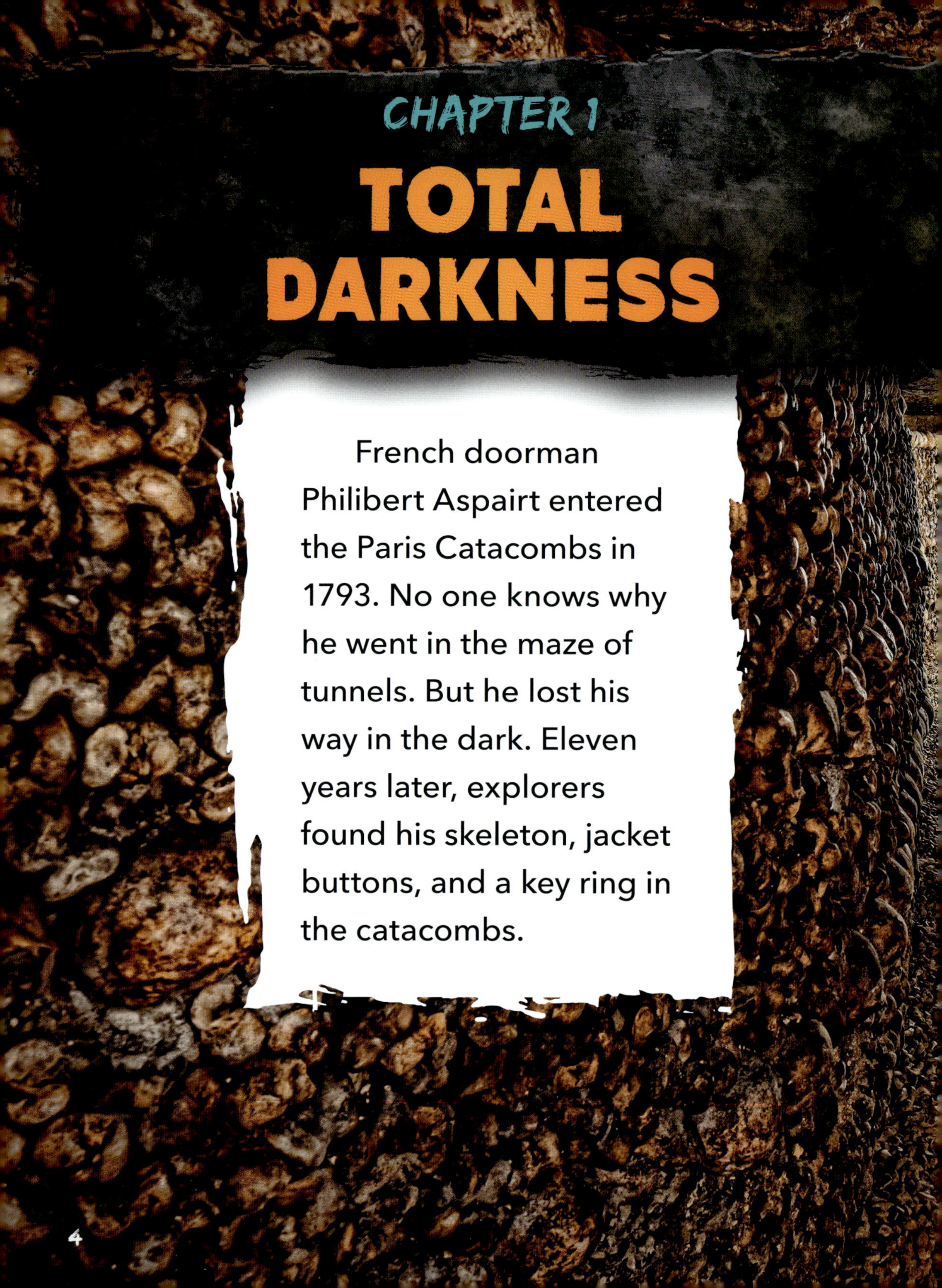

CHAPTER 1

TOTAL DARKNESS

French doorman Philibert Aspairt entered the Paris Catacombs in 1793. No one knows why he went in the maze of tunnels. But he lost his way in the dark. Eleven years later, explorers found his skeleton, jacket buttons, and a key ring in the catacombs.

Only a small part of the Paris Catacombs holds the bones of the dead.

Aspairt was buried where his body was found. A tombstone (*pictured*) was left in his memory.

CHAPTER 2

MYSTERIOUS MAZES

Explorers have found more than 2,000 mysterious tunnels under Europe. They are called erdstall tunnels. Scientists don't know when or how they were built or who built them.

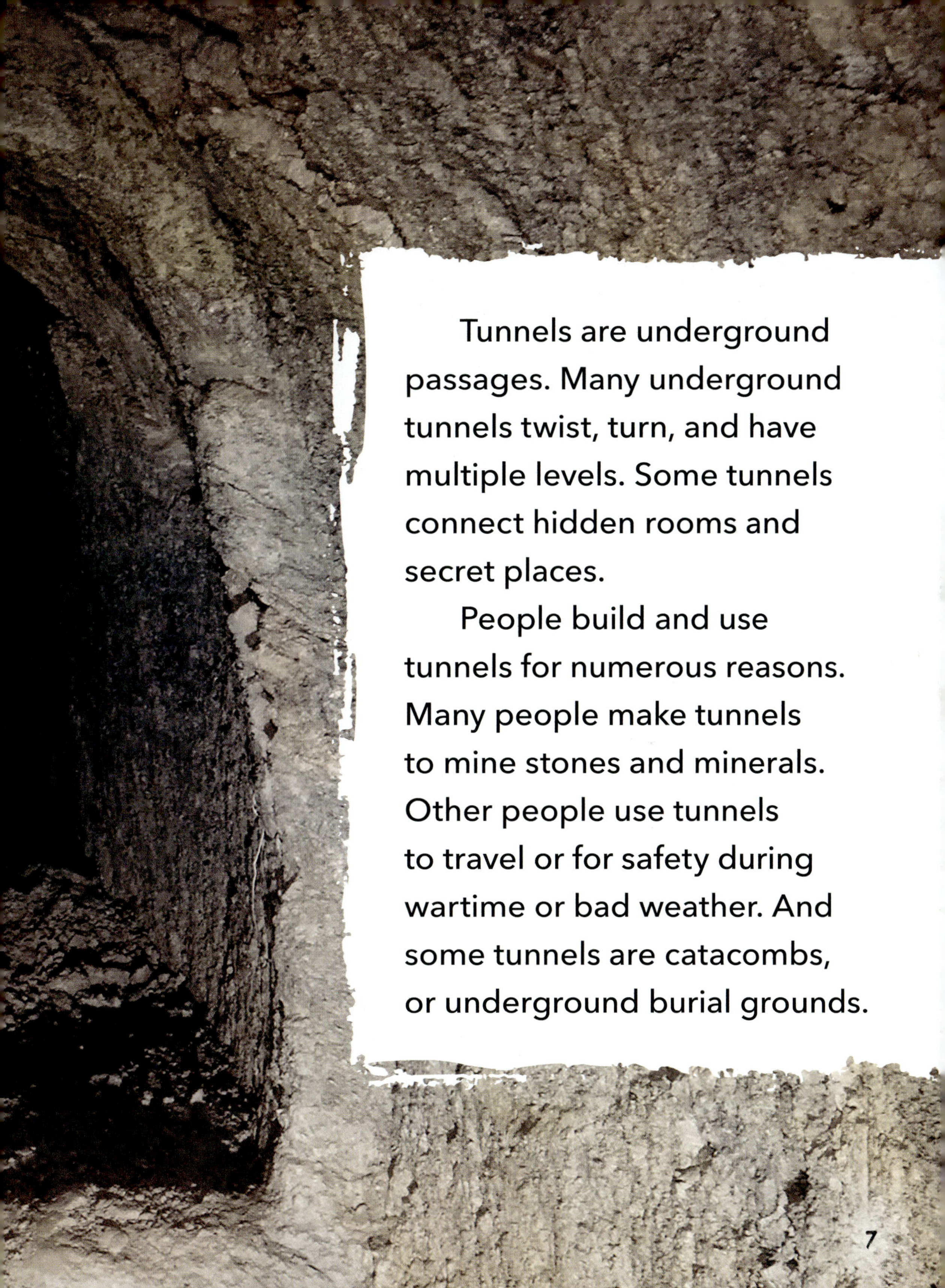

Tunnels are underground passages. Many underground tunnels twist, turn, and have multiple levels. Some tunnels connect hidden rooms and secret places.

People build and use tunnels for numerous reasons. Many people make tunnels to mine stones and minerals. Other people use tunnels to travel or for safety during wartime or bad weather. And some tunnels are catacombs, or underground burial grounds.

CHAPTER 3

PARIS CATACOMBS

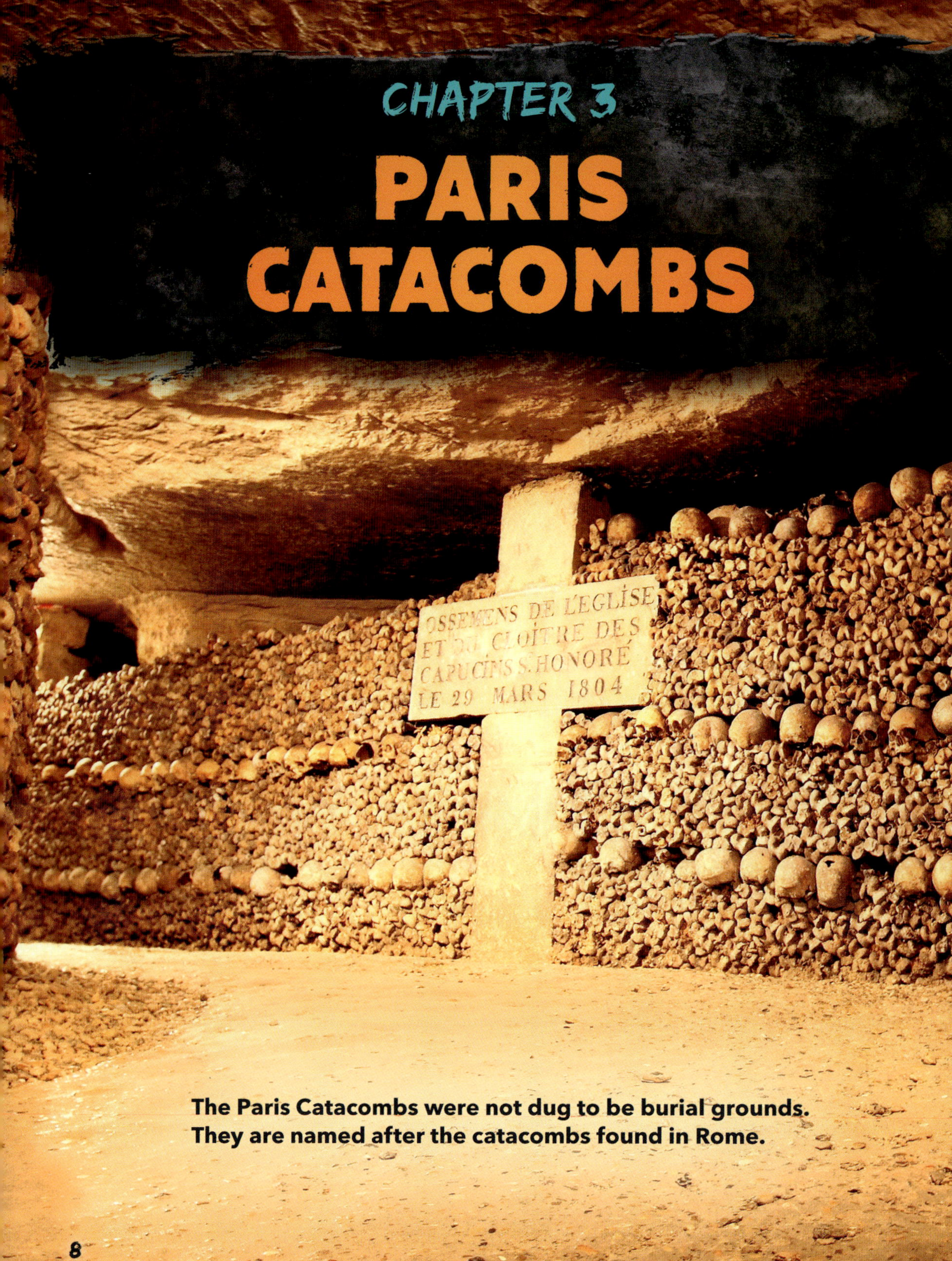

The Paris Catacombs were not dug to be burial grounds. They are named after the catacombs found in Rome.

The ground beneath Paris, France, is full of tunnels. These were originally limestone **quarries**. They were started by the Romans around 60 BCE. Over time, people created more than 180 miles (290 km) of tunnels.

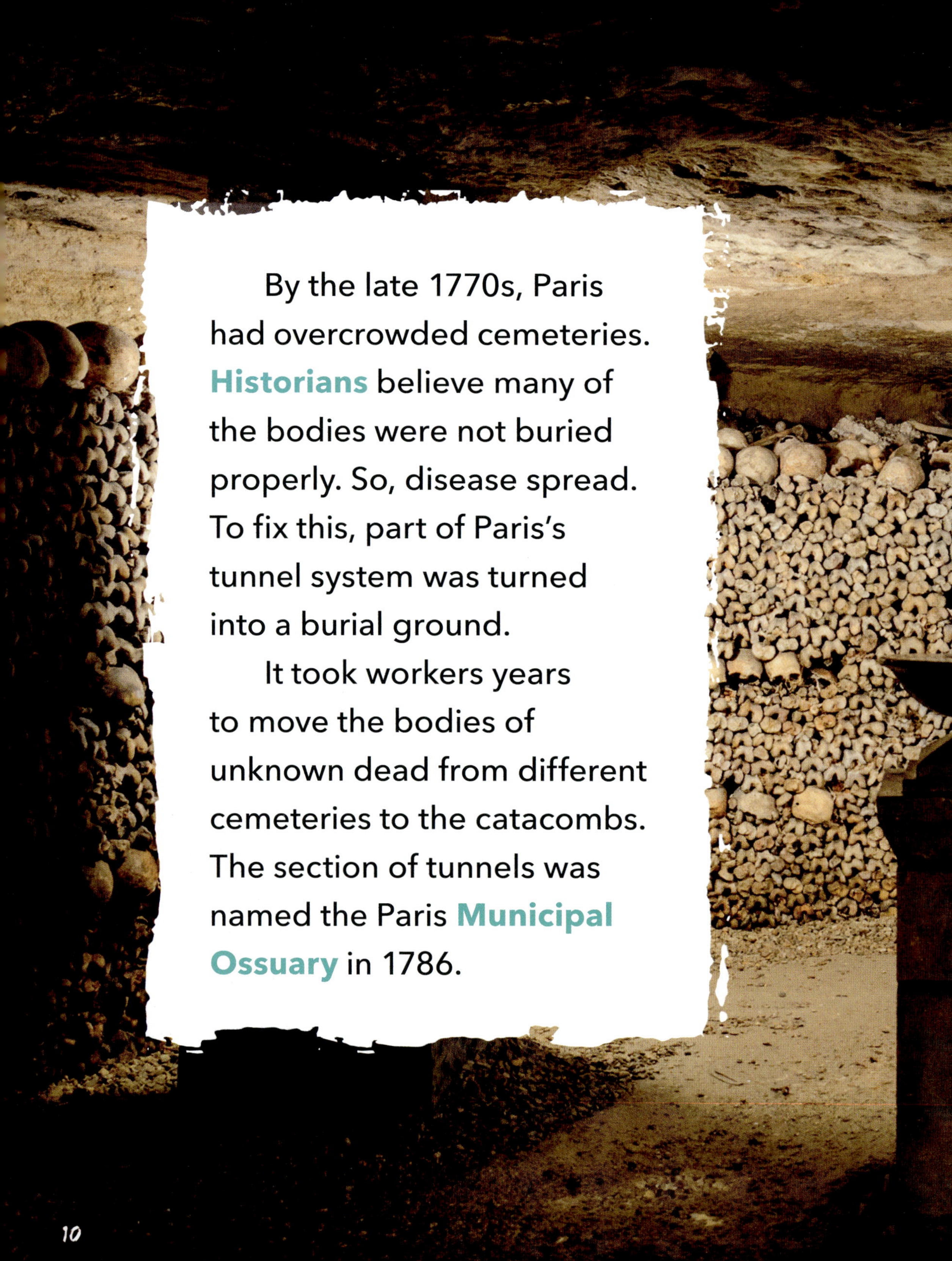

By the late 1770s, Paris had overcrowded cemeteries. **Historians** believe many of the bodies were not buried properly. So, disease spread. To fix this, part of Paris's tunnel system was turned into a burial ground.

It took workers years to move the bodies of unknown dead from different cemeteries to the catacombs. The section of tunnels was named the Paris **Municipal Ossuary** in 1786.

Workers moved more than six million bodies into the tunnels. They arranged the bones into the archways, tunnels, and walls of the catacombs.

A carving of the fortress of Port-Mahon in the Paris Catacombs. French miner François Décure secretly carved three different sculptures in the Paris Catacombs between 1777 and 1782.

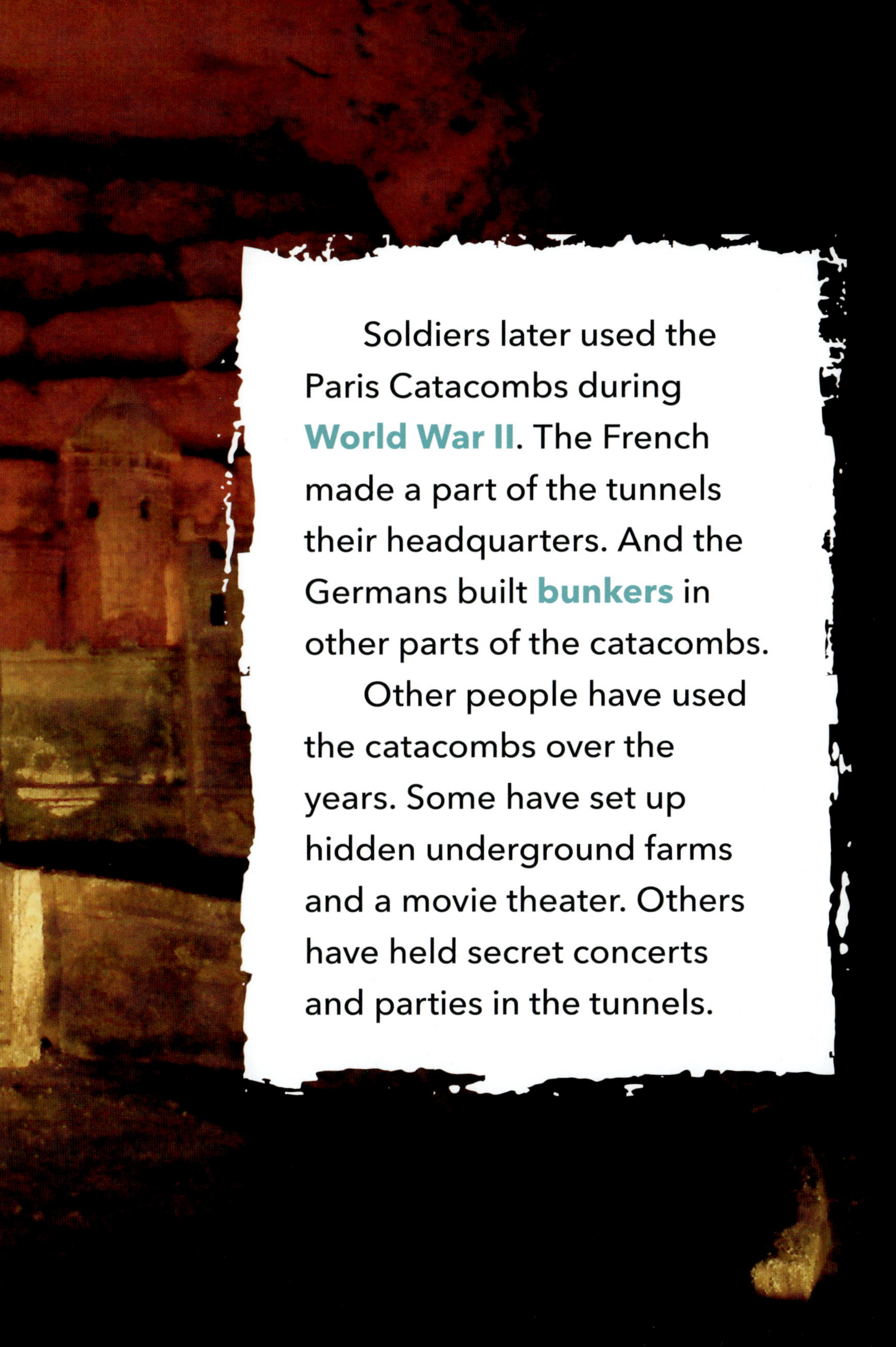

Soldiers later used the Paris Catacombs during **World War II**. The French made a part of the tunnels their headquarters. And the Germans built **bunkers** in other parts of the catacombs.

Other people have used the catacombs over the years. Some have set up hidden underground farms and a movie theater. Others have held secret concerts and parties in the tunnels.

Historians study the Paris Catacombs. They learn about Paris's history and old burial practices. **Archaeologists** work to protect the bones from **humidity**.

About one mile (1.6 km) of the Paris Municipal Ossuary was opened to the public in 1809.

XTREME FACT

Most of the Paris Catacombs are closed to the public. But people called *cataphiles* illegally explore the tunnels. Police officers called *cataflics* patrol the tunnels.

CHAPTER 4

CU CHI TUNNELS

The Cu Chi Tunnels are very small. Most measure about two feet (0.6 m) wide by three feet (0.9 m) tall.

Vietnamese soldiers started the Cu Chi Tunnels in the 1940s. This was during the **First Indochina War**. The soldiers dug tunnels and hidden rooms using hand tools. They traveled, hid, and stored supplies in the tunnels and rooms.

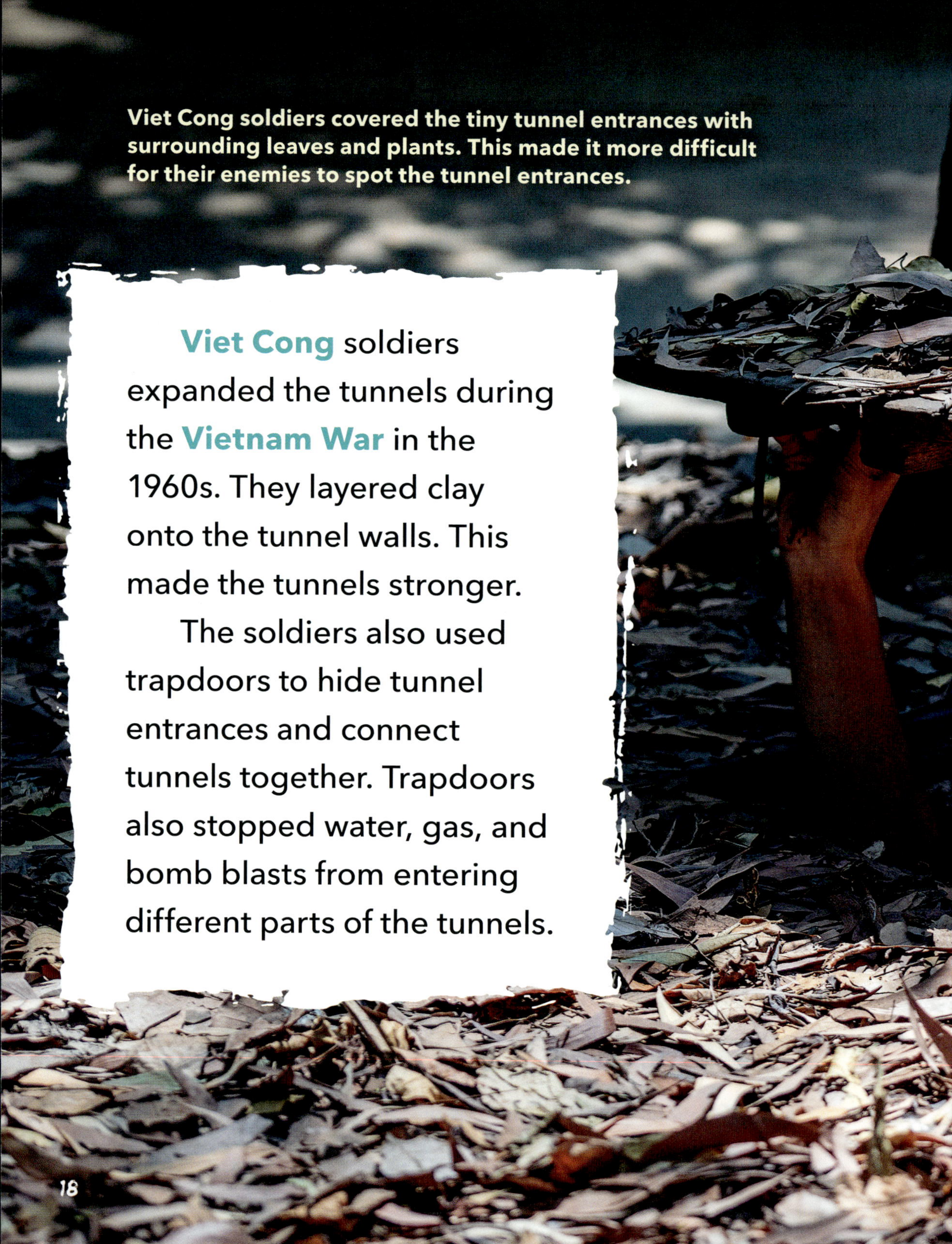

Viet Cong soldiers covered the tiny tunnel entrances with surrounding leaves and plants. This made it more difficult for their enemies to spot the tunnel entrances.

Viet Cong soldiers expanded the tunnels during the **Vietnam War** in the 1960s. They layered clay onto the tunnel walls. This made the tunnels stronger.

The soldiers also used trapdoors to hide tunnel entrances and connect tunnels together. Trapdoors also stopped water, gas, and bomb blasts from entering different parts of the tunnels.

Soldiers hid air vents by making them look like termite hills.

The **Viet Cong** built a hidden base in the tunnels. It included living quarters, kitchens, hospitals, and more. Soldiers also set deadly traps for enemies who entered the tunnels. These set off **grenades**, dropped poisonous animals, and more.

A diagram of a section of the Cu Chi Tunnels. The tunnels grew to about 155 miles (250 km) long during the Vietnam War.

XTREME FACT

US and South Vietnamese forces trained soldiers to go into the Cu Chi Tunnels. They were called “tunnel rats.” Their job was to find **Viet Cong** traps or soldiers.

The Cu Chi Tunnels can only fit one person at a time. Some were even widened to fit visitors.

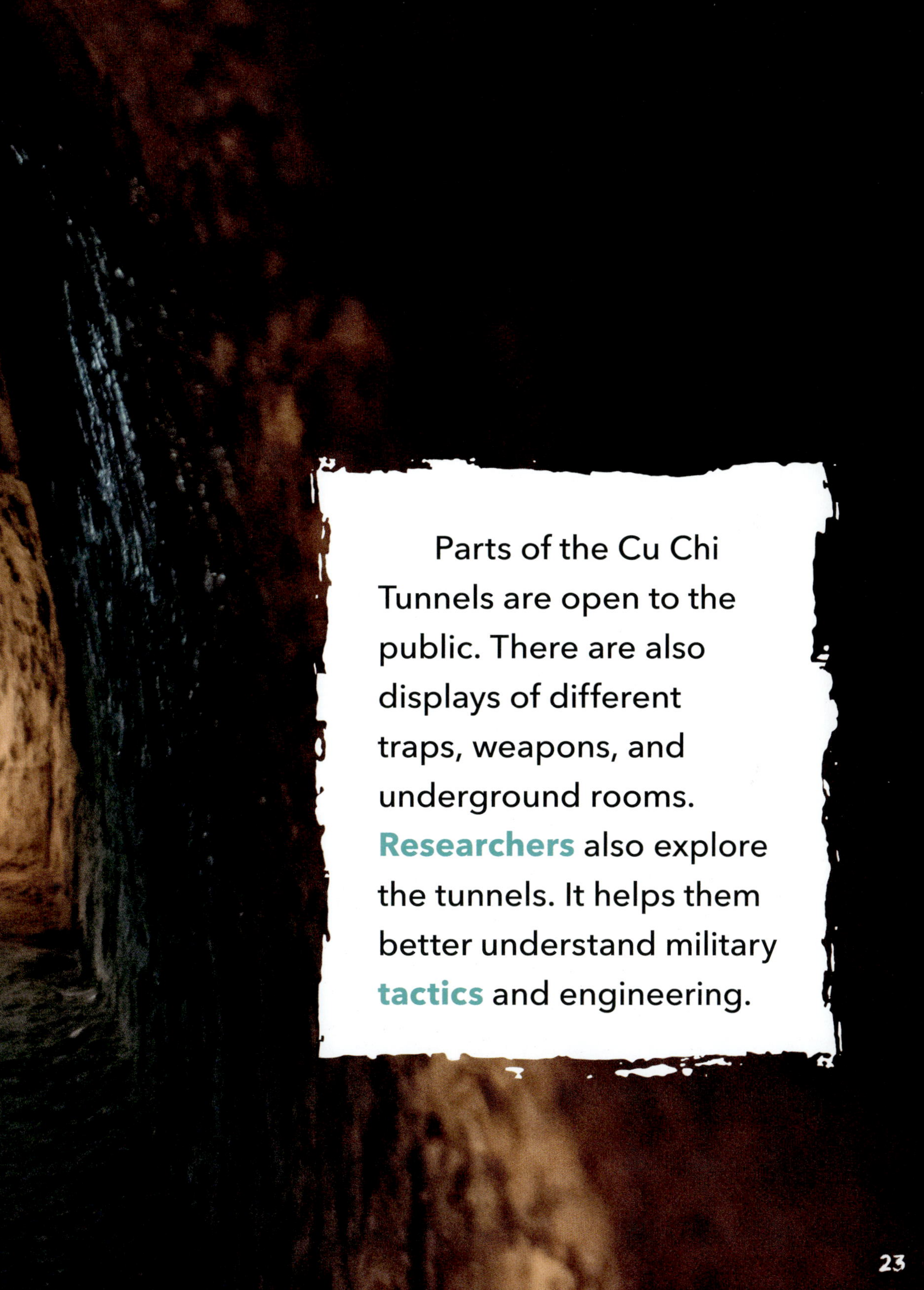

Parts of the Cu Chi Tunnels are open to the public. There are also displays of different traps, weapons, and underground rooms. **Researchers** also explore the tunnels. It helps them better understand military **tactics** and engineering.

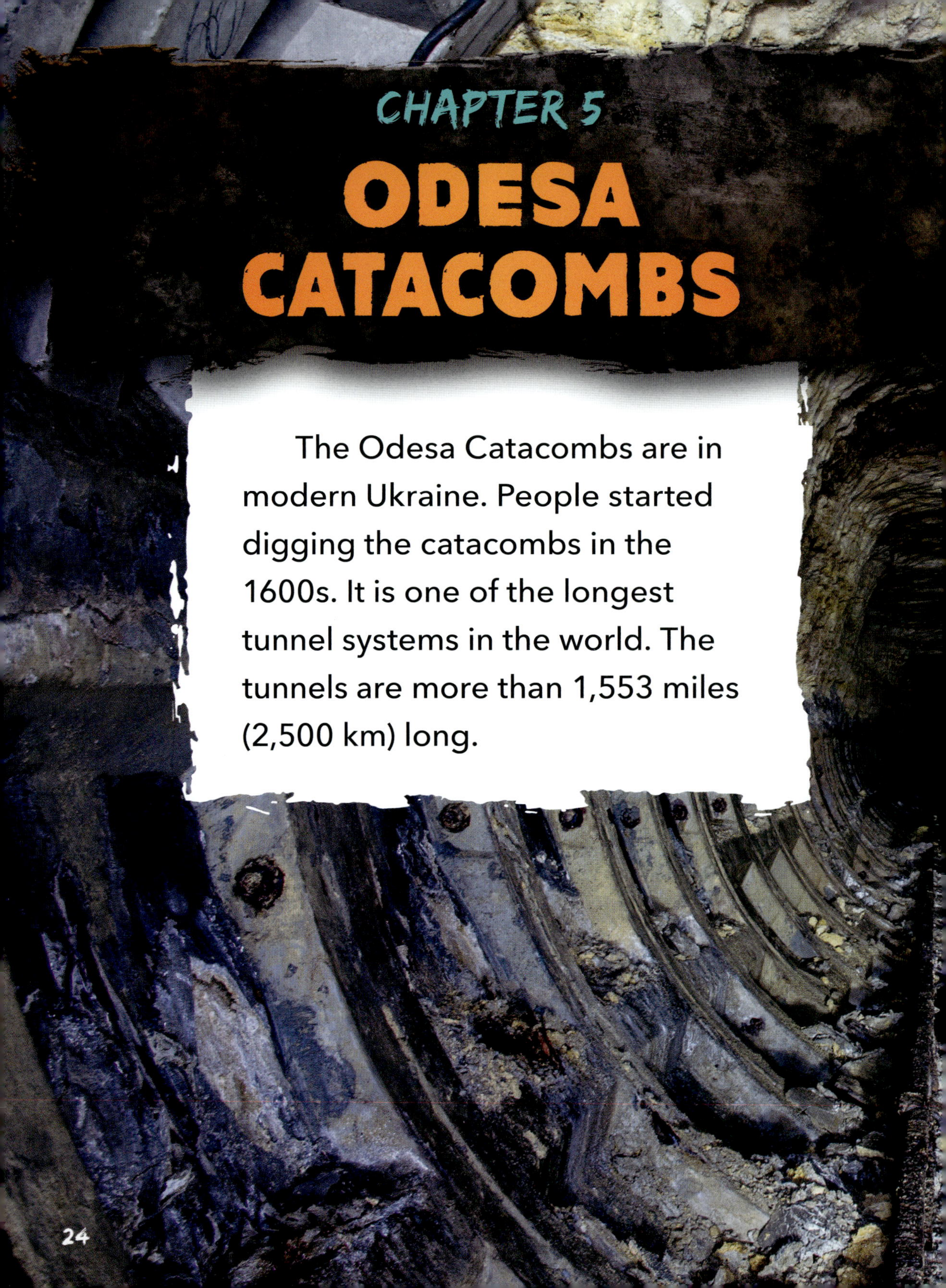

CHAPTER 5

ODESA CATACOMBS

The Odesa Catacombs are in modern Ukraine. People started digging the catacombs in the 1600s. It is one of the longest tunnel systems in the world. The tunnels are more than 1,553 miles (2,500 km) long.

People extended the Odesa Catacombs while mining a soft rock called coquina. They used coquina to build homes and palaces.

XTREME FACT

People have used the Odesa Catacombs to hide and move around in secret.

Unlike the Paris Catacombs, the Odesa Catacombs were never used to hold the dead.

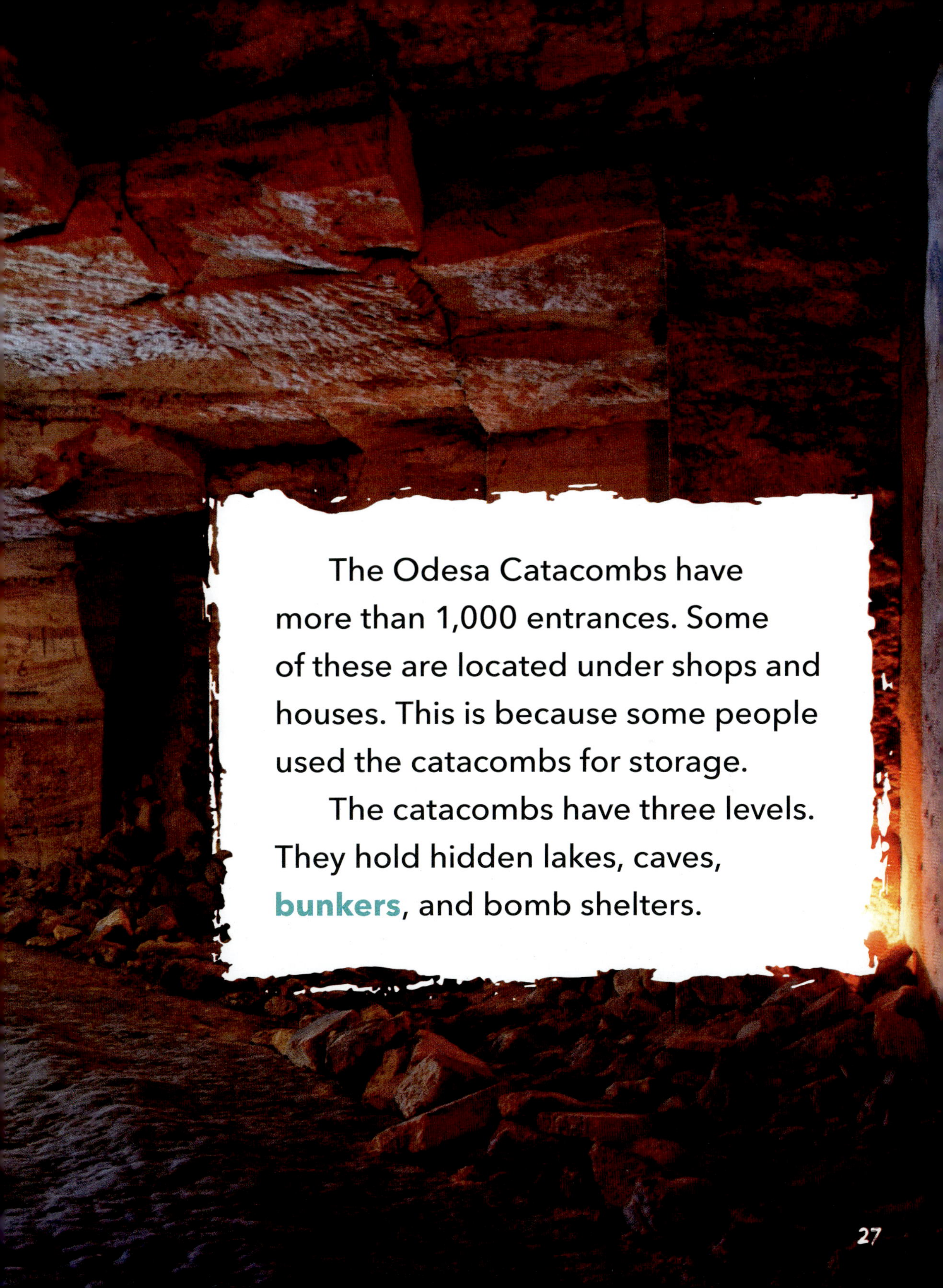

The Odesa Catacombs have more than 1,000 entrances. Some of these are located under shops and houses. This is because some people used the catacombs for storage.

The catacombs have three levels. They hold hidden lakes, caves, **bunkers**, and bomb shelters.

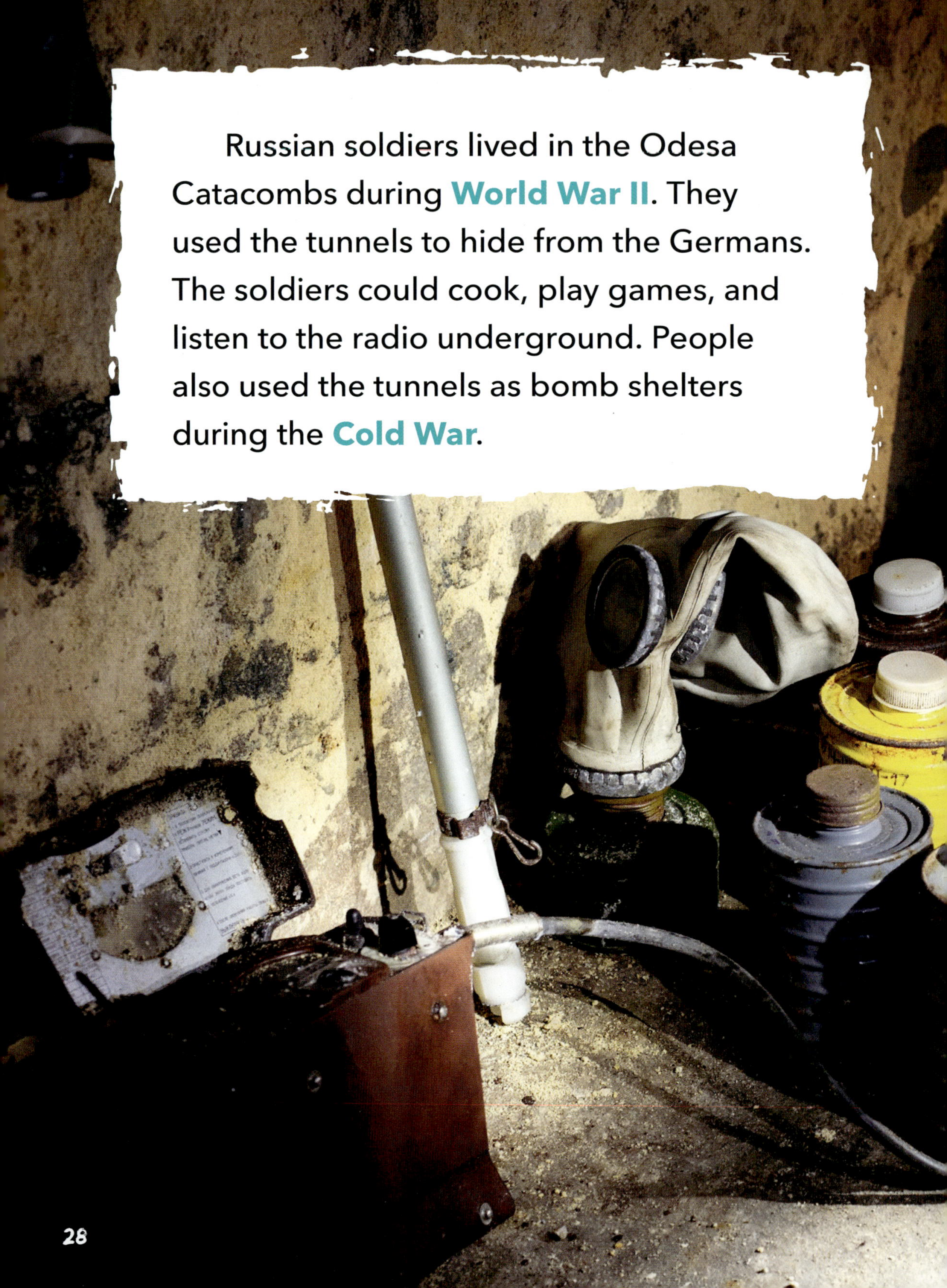

Russian soldiers lived in the Odesa Catacombs during **World War II**. They used the tunnels to hide from the Germans. The soldiers could cook, play games, and listen to the radio underground. People also used the tunnels as bomb shelters during the **Cold War**.

Many World War II and Cold War objects were left in the Odesa Catacombs.

Scientists think less than half of the caves and tunnels in the Odesa Catacombs have been explored!

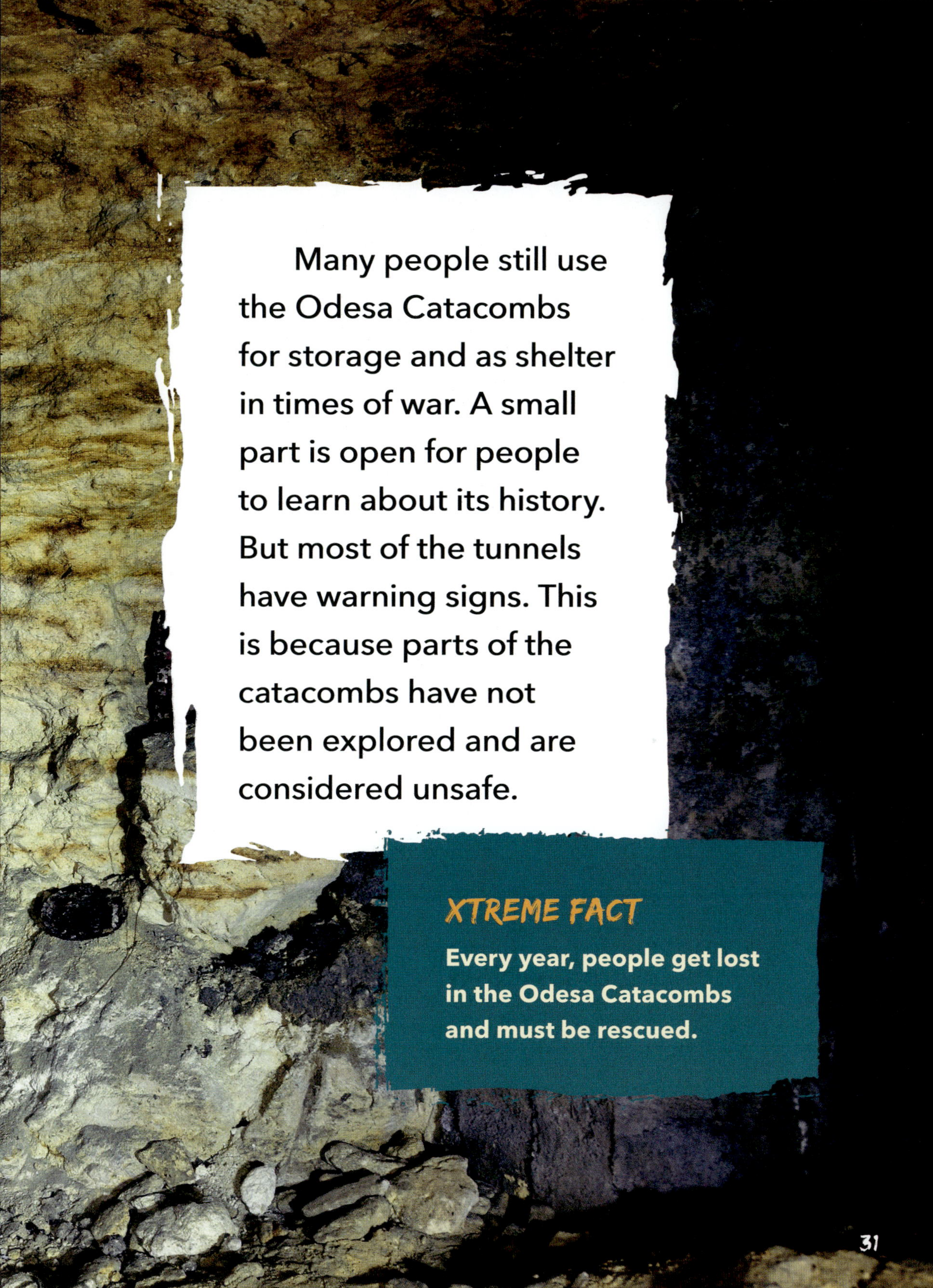

Many people still use the Odesa Catacombs for storage and as shelter in times of war. A small part is open for people to learn about its history. But most of the tunnels have warning signs. This is because parts of the catacombs have not been explored and are considered unsafe.

XTREME FACT

Every year, people get lost in the Odesa Catacombs and must be rescued.

NAPLES UNDERGROUND

The tunnels under Naples, Italy, are about 280 miles (450 km) long. They were first created by the Greeks around 300 BCE. The Greeks were digging **quarries** for a soft rock called tuff. They used tuff to build walls and temples.

One part of Naples Underground holds the Fontanelle Cemetery. This was previously an ossuary that now holds the bones of an unknown number of people.

The Romans expanded the tunnels around 20 BCE. They also built underground **aqueducts**. These supplied water to buildings and fountains.

Archaeologists also found caves, passageways, and catacombs (*pictured*) under Naples.

People later used Naples Underground as a bomb shelter during **World War II**. More than 40,000 people hid and lived there. They left objects such as cots, furniture, and cars.

XTREME FACT

Scientists created a garden in Naples Underground called The Path in 2015. The garden protects plants from pollution, acid rain, and dust.

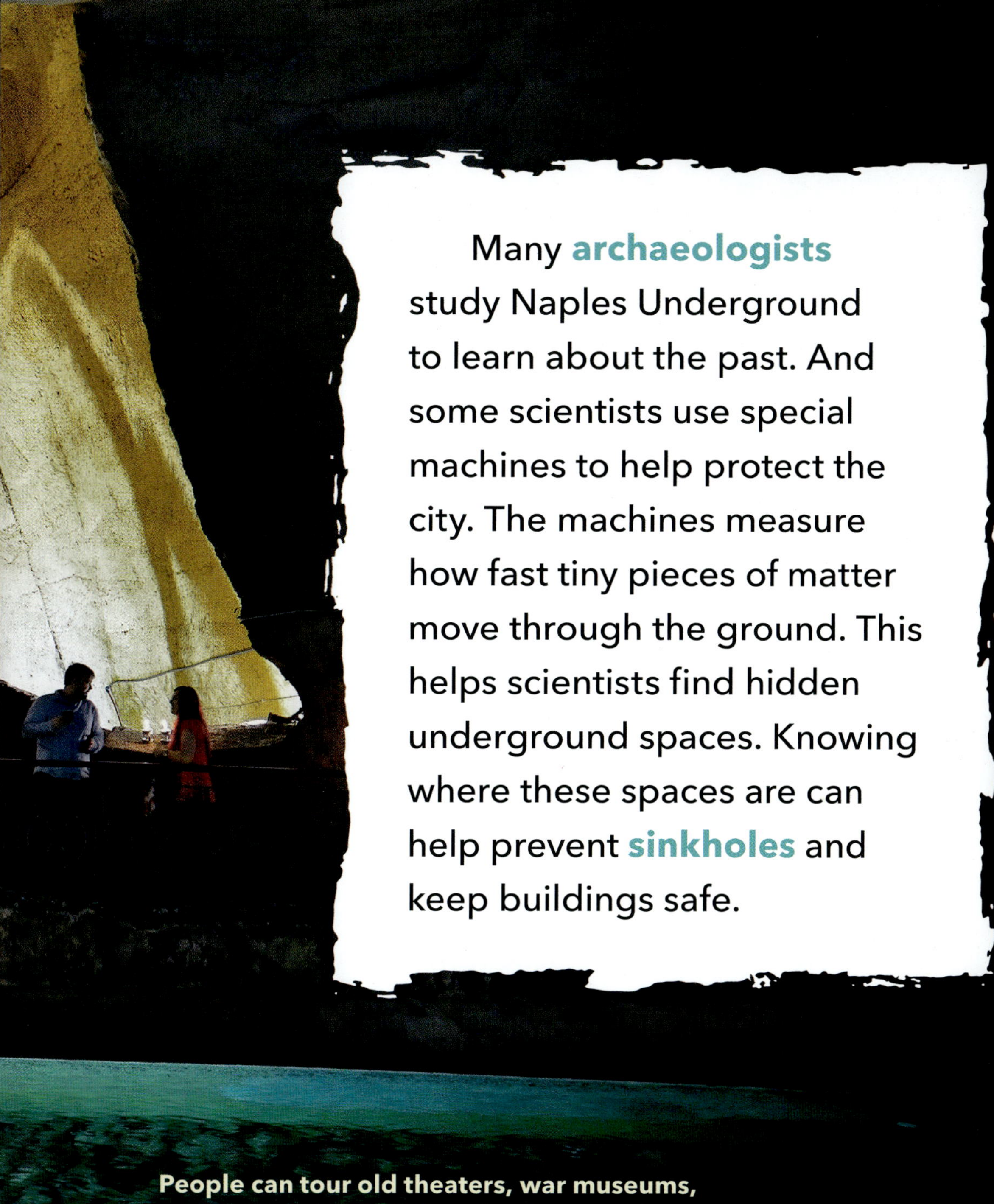

Many **archaeologists** study Naples Underground to learn about the past. And some scientists use special machines to help protect the city. The machines measure how fast tiny pieces of matter move through the ground. This helps scientists find hidden underground spaces. Knowing where these spaces are can help prevent **sinkholes** and keep buildings safe.

People can tour old theaters, war museums, and cisterns (*pictured*) under Naples.

CHAPTER 7

CHICAGO'S TUNNELS

The ground under Chicago, Illinois, is made of clay and limestone. This makes it easy for people to dig tunnels. These include water tunnels, freight tunnels, and more.

In 1864, Chicago workers began digging a tunnel under Lake Michigan. The tunnel supplied the city with clean drinking water. Over time, workers created more water tunnels. Now, around 65 miles (105 km) of tunnels bring fresh water to Chicago.

The first water tunnel was two miles (3.2 km) long. It connected Lake Michigan to a pumping station in Chicago.

A diagram drawn in 1867 shows the Lake Michigan water tunnel's progress.

In 1900, workers created almost 60 miles (97 km) of freight tunnels. Workers started using an underground railroad to travel through these tunnels in 1906. They moved coal, mail, packages, and more between different buildings in downtown Chicago.

Workers used small electric tunnel trains to deliver freight to the basements of downtown Chicago buildings.

Motor vehicles were faster and better than underground trains. So, the freight tunnels were abandoned in 1959.

XTREME FACT

There are hidden stained glass passageways and underground swimming pools along the **pedway**.

The Chicago Pedway is about 5 miles (8 km) long and covers more than 40 blocks. It also has different shops and restaurants.

The Chicago **Pedway** is another set of Chicago tunnels. The city started building the tunnels in 1951. The pedway connects 50 downtown office buildings, shopping centers, and train stations. People use it to walk under the city. It protects them during times of heavy snow or rain.

CHAPTER 8

WHAT IS HIDING UNDER YOUR FEET?

Scientists believe there are many undiscovered tunnels, passages, and catacombs worldwide. These places can help us learn about how people lived in the past. The ground beneath our feet is full of mysteries just waiting to be explored!

Visitors use stairs made of tuff to reach Naples Underground. The tunnels are at least 131 feet (40 m) deep.

XTREME CHALLENGE

TAKE THE QUIZ BELOW AND PUT WHAT YOU'VE LEARNED TO THE TEST!

1) Would you want to explore an underground catacomb or tunnel? Why or why not?

2) How would you keep from getting lost in the Odesa Catacombs?

3) If you could design secret tunnels for a big city, what would you include and why?

4) Who first dug the Paris Catacombs and why?

GLOSSARY

aqueduct–a type of canal or similar structure that carries water over long distances.

archaeologist–a person who studies the remains of ancient people and their activities.

bunker–a shelter dug into the ground to keep people safe from attack.

Cold War–a period of tension from 1945 to 1991 between the United States and the Soviet Union. They competed for power and influence without fighting each other directly.

First Indochina War–from 1946 to 1954. A war where the Vietnamese people fought for independence against France.

grenade–a small bomb that is thrown by hand or shot from a gun.

historian–a person who studies or writes about past events.

humidity–the amount of moisture in the air.

municipal ossuary–a place for the bones of the dead that is owned by the government.

pedway–a path usually built in an urban area for people to walk.

quarry–an open pit usually used for obtaining building stone, slate, or limestone.

researcher–a person who carefully studies a subject in order to learn facts about it.

sinkhole—a hole that forms in the ground when the surface collapses, often because the ground beneath it has been weakened or eroded.

tactic—a method of moving military forces in battle.

Viet Cong—a communist group from North Vietnam that fought against South Vietnam and the US during the Vietnam War.

Vietnam War—from 1954 to 1975. A long, failed attempt by the United States to stop North Vietnam from taking over South Vietnam.

World War II—from 1939 to 1945, fought in Europe, Asia, and Africa. Great Britain, France, the United States, the Soviet Union, and their allies were on one side. Germany, Italy, Japan, and their allies were on the other side.

ONLINE RESOURCES

To learn more about tunnels and passages, please visit **abdobooklinks.com** or scan this QR code. These links are routinely monitored and updated to provide the most current information available.

INDEX